St. Mary

MATTHEW 10–20

On the Road
with Jesus

A Guided Discovery for Groups and Individuals
Kevin Perrotta

LOYOLAPRESS.
CHICAGO

LOYOLAPRESS.

3441 N. ASHLAND AVENUE
CHICAGO, ILLINOIS 60657
(800) 621-1008
WWW.LOYOLABOOKS.ORG

Nihil Obstat
Reverend John G. Lodge, S.S.L., S.T.D.
Censor Deputatus
August 17, 2003

Imprimatur
Most Reverend Edwin M. Conway, D.D.
Vicar General
Archdiocese of Chicago
August 22, 2003

The *Nihil Obstat* and *Imprimatur* are official declarations that a book is free of doctrinal and moral error. No implication is contained therein that those who have granted the *Nihil Obstat* and *Imprimatur* agree with the content, opinions, or statements expressed. Nor do they assume any legal responsibility associated with publication.

The Scripture quotations contained herein are from the New Revised Standard Version Bible: Catholic Edition, copyright © 1993 and 1989 by the Division of Christian Education of the National Council of the Churches of Christ in the U.S.A. Used by permission. All rights reserved. Subheadings in Scripture quotations have been added by Kevin Perrotta.

Information about NET (National Evangelization Teams) Ministries (p. 23) can be found at www.netusa.org.

Information about Fr. Rick Thomas and Our Lady's Youth Center (p. 33) can be obtained from Our Lady's Youth Center, P.O. Box 1422, El Paso, Texas 79948; (915) 533-9122.

The prayer by Adrienne von Speyr (p. 42) is quoted from Hans Urs von Balthasar, *First Glance at Adrienne von Speyr,* Antje Lawry and Sergia Englund, O.C.D., trans. (San Francisco: Ignatius Press, 1981), 214–16.

The excerpt from the *Catechism of the Catholic Church* (p. 52) is from section 2843 (Washington, D.C.: United States Catholic Conference, 1997).

The remarks on guardian angels by St. Thomas Aquinas (p. 53) are taken from his *Summa Theologiae,* I, 111, 1–4 and I, 113, 4–5. The translation is by Dominican fathers of the English province. The full text may be viewed at www.ccel.org/a/aquinas/summa/home.html.

The quotations from Pope John Paul II's encyclical *Veritatis Splendor* (p. 65) are taken from the English translation prepared by the Holy See, which may be found at the Web site of the Holy See, www.vatican.va.

The Latin text of St. Jerome's commentary *In Matheum* (p. 75) may be found in *S. Hieronymi Presbyteri Opera,* pars I, 7, Corpus Christianorum, Series Latina, vol. 77 (Turnhout, Belgium: Typographi Brepols, 1969). Translation by Kevin Perrotta.

Interior design by Kay Hartmann/Communique Design
Illustration by Charise Mericle Harper

ISBN 0-8294-1545-9

Printed in the United States of America
04 05 06 07 08 09 10 11 Bang 10 9 8 7 6 5 4 3 2 1

Contents

How to Use This Guide

Y ou might compare the Bible to a national park. The park is so large that you could spend months, even years, getting to know it. But a brief visit, if carefully planned, can be enjoyable and worthwhile. In a few hours you can drive through the park and pull over at a handful of sites. At each stop you can get out of the car, take a short trail through the woods, listen to the wind blowing through the trees, get a feel for the place.

In this booklet, we'll drive through a small portion of the Bible—the Gospel according to Matthew—making half a dozen stops along the way. At those points we'll proceed on foot, taking a leisurely walk through the selected passages. After each discussion we'll get back in the car and take the highway to the next stop.

This guide provides everything you need to explore the readings from Matthew's Gospel in six discussions—or to do a six-part exploration on your own. The introduction on page 6 will prepare you to get the most out of your reading. The weekly sections provide explanations that highlight what the Gospel means for us today. Equally important, each section supplies questions that will launch your group into fruitful discussion, helping you to both investigate the Gospel for yourself and learn from one another. If you're using the booklet by yourself, the questions will spur your personal reflection.

Each discussion is meant to be a *guided discovery*.

Guided. None of us is equipped to read the Bible without help. We read the Bible *for* ourselves but not *by* ourselves. Scripture was written to be understood and applied in the community of faith. So each week "A Guide to the Reading," drawing on the work of both modern biblical scholars and Christian writers of the past, supplies background and explanations. The guide will help you grasp the message of Matthew's Gospel. Think of it as a friendly park ranger who points out noteworthy details and explains what you're looking at so you can appreciate things for yourself.

Discovery. The purpose is for *you* to interact with Matthew's Gospel. "Questions for Careful Reading" is a tool to help you dig into the text and examine it carefully. "Questions for Application" will help you consider what these words mean for your life here and now. Each week concludes with an "Approach to Prayer" section that helps you respond to God's word. Supplementary "Living Tradition" and "Saints in the Making" sections offer the thoughts and experiences of Christians past and present. By showing what the Gospel has meant to others, these sections will help you consider what it means for you.

How long are the discussion sessions? We've assumed you will have about an hour and a half when you get together. If you have less time, you'll find that most of the elements can be shortened somewhat.

Is homework necessary? You will get the most out of your discussions if you read the weekly material and prepare answers to the questions in advance of each meeting. If participants are not able to prepare, have someone read the "Guide to the Reading" sections aloud to the group at the points where they appear. (Note that the guide in Week 5 is twice the usual length.)

What about leadership? If you happen to have a world-class biblical scholar in your group, by all means ask him or her to lead the discussions. In the absence of any professional Scripture scholars, or even accomplished amateur biblical scholars, you can still have a first-class Bible discussion. Choose two or three people to take turns as facilitators, and have everyone read "Suggestions for Bible Discussion Groups" (page 76) before beginning.

Does everyone need a guide? a Bible? Everyone in the group will need their own copy of this booklet. It contains the text of the portions of the Gospel that are discussed in the weekly sessions, so a Bible is not absolutely necessary—but each participant will find it useful to have one. You should have at least one Bible on hand for your discussions. (See page 80 for recommendations.)

How do we get started? Before you begin, take a look at the suggestions for Bible discussion groups (page 76) or individuals (page 79).

Getting the Most out of Your Journey

The marvelous thing about the Gospels is that they bring us into contact with Jesus. Jesus' earthly life is far in the past. But through the Gospels, we can join his disciples as they accompany him along the roads of first-century Palestine, watching and listening to him. The Gospels are a meeting place where we can hear Jesus speaking to us and we can speak to him.

In this book, we are going to do just that—listen to Jesus so that we can speak to him. We're going to hit the road with Jesus. Our six readings are all taken from the accounts of Jesus' journeys with his disciples in the middle part of Matthew's Gospel.

Entering into the Gospel accounts is a simple matter. All we have to do is begin to read. But a little work is required for us to get the most out of our reading. The work is twofold. First, in order to get into the story thoroughly and grasp the significance of what Jesus is saying and doing, we need to know something about the political and religious situation in which he is operating. Then, when we leave the story and return to the twenty-first century, we need to determine how his words and example should guide us in our very different modern world.

A full-scale review of the situation of the Jewish people in the early first century would take us way beyond the limits of this short introduction. But you are probably acquainted with some of the basic facts. In Jesus' time, the Jews' ancestral land was ruled by Rome. Under the Romans, the Jews suffered both the humiliation of foreign domination and the pain of economic exploitation, which fell especially hard on the poorer inhabitants. Some Jews—such as Herod and his aristocrats, whom we will meet in our readings—benefited from cooperating with the Romans, but they were a small minority.

Of course, the situation was largely the same for other peoples in the Roman Empire. But in some respects the Jews were different from other peoples. They were convinced that God (unlike most of their neighbors, they believed in the existence of only one God) had chosen them to be his special people. Many Jews believed that God would ultimately make a grand intervention into history to free them from foreign oppression and other evils. They thought that God would gather his people, Israel, from foreign lands, wipe away their sins, and inaugurate an age of holiness, abundance, and peace.

Jewish people held varying opinions regarding how and when God would fulfill these expectations. Many expected God to send a powerful figure (or perhaps more than one) to lead the process of liberation and renewal—a man specially deputized, or "anointed," to spearhead the coming of God's kingdom through military action. The Hebrew for "Anointed One" is *Messiah;* via Greek this title has come into English as *Christ.*

The history of Palestine in the century after Jesus' death and resurrection demonstrates just how powerfully these expectations influenced Jewish people in that period. Inspired by the belief that God was about to liberate his people, as well as by economic desperation, Jews mounted two massive revolts against Rome—the greatest uprisings ever carried out by any people in the Roman Empire. Both rebellions ended in utter failure.

In some way, to some degree, many of the men and women who observed Jesus in first-century Galilee, including those who became his followers, shared these expectations of an ultimate intervention by God in the world. These expectations shaped their understanding of who Jesus was and what he was about. His displays of healing power and other miraculous deeds led them to suspect that he might be the one to accomplish God's plans (see John 6:11–15). They interpreted his announcement that God's kingdom was about to arrive (4:17—except where noted, the scriptural citations in this guide refer to the Gospel of Matthew) as a declaration that the liberation of God's people was at hand (see Luke 24:21). When Jesus instructed his disciples to take his announcement "to the lost sheep of the house of Israel" (10:6), the disciples probably understood this commission as the beginning of the gathering of God's people—the first phase of the awaited liberation. Perhaps the revolt against the Roman occupation was about to begin!

The anticipations that Jesus aroused must have been one of the major reasons why Jesus' first disciples were attracted to him. But, as we will see in our readings from Matthew's Gospel, while Jesus did encourage his disciples to recognize him as the Messiah, he also countered some of their expectations with a massive no. He revealed that he was not the kind of Messiah they had been looking for, that God's kingdom was not going to come in the way they expected it to, and that life in God's kingdom would not be exactly as they envisioned.

Jesus taught that God's kingdom would not be established through military conquest and political domination but through his own voluntary death (20:17–19, 28). Unlike earthly realms, God's kingdom would not be geared to making the powerful rich and the rich honored. It would be based on principles of love and service (20:25–27). Life in God's kingdom would not be a matter of getting but of giving, not a matter of gaining power and prestige but of relinquishing power and prestige in the process of serving other people. It would be a kingdom of unlimited forgiveness, mercy, compassion, and humble care for the socially insignificant (18:1–5, 21–35).

The difference between Jesus' understanding of his mission and his disciples' expectations created powerful crosscurrents in the relationship between the master and his disciples. The disciples accepted Jesus as their teacher—that is what it meant to be his "disciples"—but they did not receive his teaching as simply as, for example, accounting students learning principles from a business school professor. They did not advance to higher and higher levels of understanding and maturity as if riding a smoothly running escalator. Jesus urged them to follow him in a direction they did not yet understand—or even want. Given their different values, the disciples sometimes failed to understand Jesus or absorb his instruction. They balked at the first indication of impending suffering.

Jesus called his disciples to change their outlook on life. Indeed, "a change of mind" is precisely the basic meaning of the Greek word for repentance used in his keynote announcement: "Repent, for the kingdom of heaven has come near" (4:17). The middle chapters of Matthew's Gospel are marked by the drama of

Jesus' call to repentance striking against the disciples' ambivalence—their mixture of desire to follow him and resistance to basic elements of his vision. As they travel with Jesus, the disciples jockey for the best positions in his soon-to-be-established regime, on the assumption that he is bringing a kind of heaven-on-earth kingdom that, like earthly kingdoms, will be based on self-aggrandizement. The tension between Jesus and his followers extends all the way through our readings, right up to the last one, at which point Jesus is about to bring his teaching ministry to a close.

The disciples need a change of thinking, and that requires an inner transformation, a change of heart. This, however, is not something they can produce in themselves. The resource for this personal transformation is, of course, Jesus himself. But in the central portion of Matthew's Gospel, this message is hinted at rather than stated directly. Perhaps the broadest hint lies in Jesus' healing miracles, which demonstrate his creative power to make damaged human beings whole.

It is in the sequel to our readings—in the final eight chapters of the Gospel—that Matthew shows more clearly that Jesus is the source of the change of heart that his disciples need. At his last meal with his disciples, Jesus indicates that he is about to voluntarily offer his life as a sacrifice to forgive sins and create a new bond, or "covenant," between God and human beings (26:26–28). This renewed relationship with God will be the source of deep inner change. Rising from death, Jesus becomes permanently, if invisibly, present among his followers (28:18–20). The risen Jesus himself will be the resource for all who seek to embrace the lifestyle of God's kingdom. He is "God is with us" (1:23).

When we return from our travels with Jesus in the Gospel to our lives in the twenty-first century, we are challenged to act on what we have seen and heard. With some of Jesus' instructions, the process of application is fairly straightforward. Jesus' directive that we should put ourselves in a posture of service to our neighbor is transparently simple. Of course, it is difficult too, but the difficulty lies in putting it into practice, not in understanding what the principle means.

Others of Jesus' instructions, however, require further pondering before they can be applied to our present situations. In the Gospel, for example, Jesus leads a life of deliberate poverty (8:20) and calls his disciples to leave everything behind and accompany him on the road (19:21). He invites them to renounce not only possessions but also marriage (19:11–12). He sends them out as missionaries with the command to maintain a strict level of material poverty and depend entirely on the hospitality of those who welcome them (10:9–11). How, if at all, do these instructions apply to Jesus' disciples in later, different situations?

The challenge of drawing guidance for Christian living from Jesus' example and instructions began as soon as he died and rose from the dead. Obviously, once Jesus was no longer physically present, it was no longer possible to be his follower by joining him as he walked from town to town in Palestine.

Matthew's Gospel reflects a very early stage in the process of determining how to apply Jesus' teaching to changing circumstances. Matthew probably composed his Gospel about fifty years after Jesus' death and resurrection. Most likely he wrote for communities of Christians from a Jewish background living somewhere in northern Palestine and Syria (what is today northern Israel, Syria, Lebanon, and southern Turkey). Many of these Jewish Christians lived in towns and villages like those that Jesus visited during his preaching tours of Galilee. Some even spoke the same language that Jesus spoke—Aramaic. Thus the Christians for whom Matthew was writing were applying Jesus' teaching in a setting quite similar to that in which he had taught his original disciples.

From evidence outside Matthew's Gospel, it seems that some of Matthew's readers continued to imitate Jesus' lifestyle and follow his instructions fairly literally, living a wandering, evangelistic life. Scholars surmise that some Christians in the Christian communities of the time lived this way for at least a period of their lives.

Yet in Matthew's day the Church was evolving from a traveling band of disciples to a settled community. Many Christians stayed at home with their families, farmed the land, raised livestock, worked at trades. They had to adapt to their own situation Jesus' instructions to leave everything behind and follow him and to go out preaching his message without any material provisions. Rather than writing off Jesus' instructions as directed only to other, freer, unmarried members of the community, they found ways to wholeheartedly serve the coming of God's kingdom within their more settled life. They used their material resources to care for the needy. They trusted in God's care for them without selling all and taking off down the road.

This process of pondering Jesus' instructions and the example of his life and then discovering ways of following him in new situations has continued through the centuries. In the course of Christian history, a wide variety of responses to Jesus' message and example has arisen. Christians have developed diverse ways to forgo possessions and family life, embrace poverty, and make themselves fully available to Jesus for service in God's kingdom. Some Christians who have chosen not to marry have pursued lives of prayer and poverty at home, in secluded places, and in monastic communities; others have created religious orders for advancing God's kingdom through myriad forms of service to the needy. At the same time, Christians who have married, raised children, worked at ordinary occupations, and taken part in shaping culture and politics have found a multitude of ways to act on Jesus' teaching.

As twenty-first-century readers of Matthew's Gospel, we enter into this tradition. Some of us will hear Jesus' words as a summons to set aside the option of marriage and career and to follow him in some form of single life and material renunciation. But the rest of us are challenged to take Jesus' example and instructions as addressed to us also. Because of the great differences between the situation of Jesus' first disciples and our situation as his twenty-first-century disciples, we have some hard work to do in determining how his words apply to our lives today. As the author of this guide, I have to struggle with these questions myself. As a reader of Matthew's Gospel, so do you. In the Questions for Application in the weekly sessions, I have suggested some questions to spur your thinking on this. May the Holy Spirit guide you as you consider what Jesus' words mean for you, given your particular circumstances and call from God.

Matthew has given us a Gospel that is rich in meaning. One aspect of his account where this wealth of meaning is on display is his portrayal of the Twelve—Jesus' inner circle of disciples—who play a large part in our readings (10:1–5; 11:1; 20:17).

On one level, by their number the Twelve symbolize the identity of the community that Jesus gathers around himself. They correspond to the twelve tribes of Israel (19:28), thus indicating that Jesus is restoring the people of Israel.

On another level, the Twelve are the embryonic leadership group for Jesus' community after his death and resurrection. As the leaders of Jesus' future community, they have a dual role. First, having been the most intimate observers of Jesus, they can present knowledgeable, credible testimony about him. Thus they are the link between Jesus and all future generations of Christians. Second, they give the basic shape to Christian teaching and to the order of the Church. While the first function is historically unique—there will never be another set of witnesses of Jesus' earthly life, death, and resurrection—the second function is one that the Twelve pass on to new leaders. As the Church grows, a succession of leaders develops. The teaching and governing authority that Jesus gave to the Twelve is exercised by their authorized successors from century to century. These are the bishops and, in a special way, the bishop of Rome, who carries on the role of Peter.

The Twelve have a third level of meaning for us. They are not only revered figures of the past, the "apostles" (10:2), the foundation stones of Jesus' community; they are also, simply, his "disciples" (10:1), that is, his learner-followers. As apostles, the Twelve are objects of veneration. As disciples, they are our representatives in the story, our stand-ins. By identifying with them we can enter the story and, like them, encounter Jesus. Through them, we ourselves speak with Jesus.

At the point where our readings from Matthew's Gospel begin, Jesus is well launched into his public ministry. Matthew does not give time indicators to enable us to determine how long Jesus has been preaching and healing. But in the Gospel passages that lead up to our readings, Matthew has already offered a great deal of information about Jesus. He has recounted a considerable sequence of events: Jesus' baptism, his initial announcement that God's kingdom is near, and his calling of disciples (chapters 3–4). He has shown Jesus giving extensive teaching to crowds and disciples in a sermon on a hillside—the Sermon on the Mount—in which Matthew has probably drawn together elements of Jesus' teaching from many times and places (chapters 5–7). He has shown Jesus engaged in constant encounters with crowds of people who seek healing from him and are interested in his preaching about God's kingdom. And he has also shown us the first signs of opposition to Jesus developing among the religious leaders (chapters 8–9).

These events set the stage for the central section of the Gospel, from which our readings are taken. In our readings, we will mostly see Jesus on the road, traveling from town to town in Galilee (the northern portion of the modern state of Israel—chapters 10–18) and then journeying south to Jerusalem, apparently taking a route on the east side of the Jordan River (in the modern kingdom of Jordan—chapters 19–20). Along the way, Jesus continues to be mobbed by people seeking healing, although increasingly he devotes his time to teaching his disciples, in preparation for his death and for their continuation of his work after his resurrection.

In our final reading, Jesus has crossed over to the west side of the Jordan River and is passing through Jericho (in the Palestinian territories today). This is his last stop before Jerusalem. There he will complete his public and private instruction, celebrate the Passover with his disciples, allow himself to be arrested and put to death, and rise triumphant from the dead.

TRAVEL LIGHT, MY FRIENDS

Questions to Begin

15 minutes
Use a question or two to get warmed up for the reading.

1 What is the most interesting course or training program you've ever taken part in?

2 Describe (briefly!) the most difficult trip you've ever taken. Would you do it again?

Opening the Bible

5 minutes
*Read the passage aloud. Let individuals take turns reading
paragraphs.*

The Reading: Matthew 9:35–38; 10:1–33, 40–42; 11:1

Being Sent by Jesus

35 Jesus went about all the cities and villages, teaching in their
synagogues, and proclaiming the good news of the kingdom, and
curing every disease and every sickness. 36 When he saw the crowds, he
had compassion for them, because they were harassed and helpless, like
sheep without a shepherd. 37 Then he said to his disciples, "The harvest
is plentiful, but the laborers are few; 38 therefore ask the Lord of the
harvest to send out laborers into his harvest."

10:1 Then Jesus summoned his twelve disciples and gave them
authority over unclean spirits, to cast them out, and to cure every
disease and every sickness. 2 These are the names of the twelve
apostles: first, Simon, also known as Peter, and his brother Andrew;
James son of Zebedee, and his brother John; 3 Philip and
Bartholomew; Thomas and Matthew the tax collector; James son of
Alphaeus, and Thaddaeus; 4 Simon the Cananaean, and Judas
Iscariot, the one who betrayed him.

5 These twelve Jesus sent out with the following instructions: "Go
nowhere among the Gentiles, and enter no town of the Samaritans,
6 but go rather to the lost sheep of the house of Israel. 7 As you go,
proclaim the good news, 'The kingdom of heaven has come near.'
8 Cure the sick, raise the dead, cleanse the lepers, cast out demons."

Imitating Jesus

"You received without payment; give without payment. 9 Take no gold,
or silver, or copper in your belts, 10 no bag for your journey, or two
tunics, or sandals, or a staff; for laborers deserve their food. 11 Whatever
town or village you enter, find out who in it is worthy, and stay there
until you leave. 12 As you enter the house, greet it. 13 If the house is
worthy, let your peace come upon it; but if it is not worthy, let your
peace return to you. 14 If anyone will not welcome you or listen to your
words, shake off the dust from your feet as you leave that house or
town. 15 Truly I tell you, it will be more tolerable for the land of Sodom
and Gomorrah on the day of judgment than for that town.

16 "See, I am sending you out like sheep into the midst of
wolves; so be wise as serpents and innocent as doves. 17 Beware of

them, for they will hand you over to councils and flog you in their synagogues; 18 and you will be dragged before governors and kings because of me, as a testimony to them and the Gentiles. 19 When they hand you over, do not worry about how you are to speak or what you are to say; for what you are to say will be given to you at that time; 20 for it is not you who speak, but the Spirit of your Father speaking through you. 21 Brother will betray brother to death, and a father his child, and children will rise against parents and have them put to death; 22 and you will be hated by all because of my name. But the one who endures to the end will be saved. 23 When they persecute you in one town, flee to the next; for truly I tell you, you will not have gone through all the towns of Israel before the Son of Man comes.

24 "A disciple is not above the teacher, nor a slave above the master; 25 it is enough for the disciple to be like the teacher, and the slave like the master. If they have called the master of the house Beelzebul, how much more will they malign those of his household! . . .

28 "Do not fear those who kill the body but cannot kill the soul; rather fear him who can destroy both soul and body in hell. 29 Are not two sparrows sold for a penny? Yet not one of them will fall to the ground apart from your Father. 30 And even the hairs of your head are all counted. 31 So do not be afraid; you are of more value than many sparrows.

32 "Everyone therefore who acknowledges me before others, I also will acknowledge before my Father in heaven; 33 but whoever denies me before others, I also will deny before my Father in heaven. . . ."

Receiving Those Jesus Sends

40 "Whoever welcomes you welcomes me, and whoever welcomes me welcomes the one who sent me. 41 Whoever welcomes a prophet in the name of a prophet will receive a prophet's reward; and whoever welcomes a righteous person in the name of a righteous person will receive the reward of the righteous; 42 and whoever gives even a cup of cold water to one of these little ones in the name of a disciple— truly I tell you, none of these will lose their reward."

11:1 Now when Jesus had finished instructing his twelve disciples, he went on from there to teach and proclaim his message in their cities.

Questions for Careful Reading

10 minutes
Choose questions according to your interest and time.

1   The disciples are urged to pray for evangelistic and pastoral workers (9:38). Is their prayer answered?

2   How would you explain Jesus' statement in 10:30?

3   What does it mean to "acknowledge" Jesus (10:32)? to "deny" him (10:33)?

4   How many different persons or groups are referred to in 10:40?

5   How much success does Jesus lead his disciples to expect in the mission on which he is sending them?

6   How do you think the disciples felt at the end of Jesus' instruction in chapter 10? (How do you feel?)

A Guide to the Reading

If participants have not read this section already, read it aloud. Otherwise go on to "Questions for Application."

9:35–10:7. Centuries before Jesus, God brought the people of Israel into existence. Now God has come among them in Jesus, who is "God is with us" (1:23). These chosen people are Jesus' first priority (10:5–6). He feels compassion for them (9:36). Everything about Jesus' approach to his mission expresses faithfulness.

Matthew lists the apostles in pairs (10:2–4). Teamwork, rather than working alone, is the norm in Jesus' service.

10:8–15. Jesus highlights the importance of his followers leaving everything behind with a triple statement: no gold, no silver, no copper (10:9). His remark about laborers deserving their food (10:10) is a way of saying that the disciples are entitled to accept bed and board from their hosts but should decline further compensation.

By setting out on their missionary journey without supplies the disciples will demonstrate their trust in God—and will give God the opportunity to show his care for them. Their message is that God is a totally dependable Father (see 6:25–34). Who will believe that message if the messengers themselves do not trust in God's fatherly care? By not acquiring anything along the way, the disciples will show that their purpose is not to enrich or empower themselves but to benefit the people to whom they preach. Unlike the original disciples, few of us are called to live in stark poverty as we go about our service to the Lord. Yet he summons us also to rely on his help and to serve others for their sake rather than our own.

Jesus' command to use his healing power is not to be overlooked (10:8). His healing power continues to be operative in the Church through the sacrament of anointing and through less formal prayers. God answers prayers for healing as he wills— sometimes miraculously, sometimes in hidden ways, sometimes through natural processes, medical treatment, and ordinary care.

10:16–33. Biblical scholar David E. Garland points out that "Jesus does not promise to protect the sheep so that they will not be harmed or to destroy the wolves before them. The disciples are given authority to cast out demons and to heal every disease, but not to fend off persecution. There are no safe-conduct passes for their mission."

Jesus' warning might raise the disciples' anxieties. Significantly, the first fear that he addresses is not their concern for their own well-being but their concern that they might not be able to carry out his mission effectively (10:19–20). Don't worry about whether you will know how to bear witness to me, Jesus says. God's Spirit will help you. ("It is not you . . . but the Spirit of your Father speaking" is a way of saying "not *only* you but *also* the Spirit"; for a similar way of speaking, see 9:13). Thus we should not let our feelings of inadequacy prevent us from speaking about Jesus when opportunities present themselves.

St. Jerome suggested a playful interpretation of 10:23: When adversaries of Christian teaching "persecute" us in one city, that is, in one book of the Scriptures, let us flee to other cities, that is, to other books, to defend our cause. No matter how argumentative our opponents may be, the help of the Savior will arrive before we have made our way through all the books of the Bible.

Jesus' advice is to trump fear of opposition with fear of turning away from God, the source of our life (10:28). Jesus warns that judgment will befall those who abandon him and his mission (10:33), but along with fear of God's judgment goes the comfort of knowing that the one who will judge us is the one who now leads us on the road—Jesus, God-is-with-us.

Jesus reassures us that if we are on a mission for him, God will be with us and will hold our entire lives in his hands (10:29–31). He does not explain how God's care works or what exactly God will provide for us. We trust God not because we can understand how he acts or what he will do for us but because he is our Father.

10:40–11:1. Jesus has been speaking to his disciples as though all of them will be wandering missionaries seeking hospitality. Now he speaks as though they will be householders who welcome wandering missionaries. The wandering ones and the stay-at-homes are members of the same community of followers. Jesus is present in all. Even the smallest service to anyone who is identified with Jesus is a service to him.

Questions for Application

40 minutes
Choose questions according to your interest and time.

1 Jesus counsels prayer before he gives his instructions about how to serve in God's kingdom (9:38). What is the role of prayer in serving God?

2 How has God's faithfulness made a difference in your life? To whom is God calling you to be faithful?

3 Who are the fellow disciples Jesus has given you? How is he calling you to cooperate with them in sharing his kingdom with others?

4 What does it mean today to proclaim that "the kingdom of heaven has come near" (10:7)? How and where do those of us who do not work full-time in the Church proclaim the kingdom of heaven?

5 How does the Church today carry out the work that Jesus gives to his disciples in 10:8? How do you take part in this work? How is Jesus calling you to be an instrument of his compassion to those in need?

6 When have you felt challenged by God to rely more directly on him? How did you respond to the challenge? What was the outcome and what have you learned from it?

7 When have you surprised yourself by speaking a truth or giving advice that seemed perfectly suited to the situation and person you were speaking to? Could this have been an experience of what Jesus predicts in 10:20? What might you learn from this incident?

8 When have you been afraid to do something that you felt God wanted you to do? What helped you deal with your fear? Have you applied this lesson to other situations in your life?

When people share with one another what they are discovering, it becomes clear that the Bible is full of endless meanings and applications.

Steve Mueller, *The Seeker's Guide to Reading the Bible*

Approach to Prayer

15 minutes
Use this approach—or create your own!

◆ Let one participant read aloud the following statements by Jesus. After each statement, pause for silent prayer and then let the group pray together, "Lord, send us wherever you wish and be with us in whatever work you give us to do."

9:37–38
10:7
10:16
10:19–20
10:30–31
10:32
10:41–42

At the end, pray the Our Father together.

Saints in the Making

Literally on the Road, for a While

This section is a supplement for individual reading.

Jesus' instructions to his disciples to go out into the world announcing the coming of God's kingdom have spurred Christians to explore a wide variety of methods for spreading his message. An obstacle to creativity here is either-or thinking, that is, that spreading the gospel means either making a lifetime commitment to full-time missionary work or bearing witness to Christ by leading an ordinary life—being married, raising children, earning a living, and taking care of household chores.

But there are options outside this either-or. One organization that has come up with a different approach is National Evangelization Teams Ministries, known as NET. Based in St. Paul, Minnesota, NET enlists and trains young adults for a one-year commitment to full-time evangelization.

Ranging in age from eighteen to thirty, NET volunteers take a year off school or work to go out in teams visiting Catholic parishes, schools, and youth groups around the United States, Canada, and Australia. In presentations and retreats that run from three hours to three days, the teams use drama, personal stories, music, and other activities to bring to young people an invitation to a personal relationship with Jesus.

Each team consists of about ten volunteers who travel in a van together, accepting hospitality from parishes and families in towns where they give their presentations. Currently, twelve teams crisscross the United States and Canada each year.

Volunteers put other aspects of their lives on hold during their year of service. They receive only a tiny stipend and have to raise money to help pay for the five-week training program (NET gives them health coverage). They agree not to date during their service year.

Since 1981, NET volunteers have given presentations to and led retreats for almost a million and a half young people. The impact of their efforts is difficult to measure, but stories of young lives touched by God's grace abound. One indication of NET's success is simply that schools and parishes keep inviting them back.

Certainly the year of service has an effect on the volunteers themselves. Almost all of those who continue as laypeople go on to serve actively in their parishes. A sizable minority decide to make a lifelong commitment to religious life or the priesthood.

MIRACLES ON TURF AND SURF

Questions to Begin

15 minutes
Use a question or two to get warmed up for the reading.

1 Do you like to dance? (What kind?) Do you like to watch dancing? (What kind?)

2 Describe a time when you really wanted to be alone.

Opening the Bible

5 minutes
Read the passage aloud. Let individuals take turns reading paragraphs.

The Reading: Matthew 14

The Death of a Prophet

[1] At that time Herod the ruler heard reports about Jesus; [2] and he said to his servants, "This is John the Baptist; he has been raised from the dead, and for this reason these powers are at work in him." [3] For Herod had arrested John, bound him, and put him in prison on account of Herodias, his brother Philip's wife, [4] because John had been telling him, "It is not lawful for you to have her." [5] Though Herod wanted to put him to death, he feared the crowd, because they regarded him as a prophet. [6] But when Herod's birthday came, the daughter of Herodias danced before the company, and she pleased Herod [7] so much that he promised on oath to grant her whatever she might ask. [8] Prompted by her mother, she said, "Give me the head of John the Baptist here on a platter." [9] The king was grieved, yet out of regard for his oaths and for the guests, he commanded it to be given; [10] he sent and had John beheaded in the prison. [11] The head was brought on a platter and given to the girl, who brought it to her mother. [12] His disciples came and took the body and buried it; then they went and told Jesus.

Miracle on the Way to Prayer

[13] Now when Jesus heard this, he withdrew from there in a boat to a deserted place by himself. But when the crowds heard it, they followed him on foot from the towns. [14] When he went ashore, he saw a great crowd; and he had compassion for them and cured their sick. [15] When it was evening, the disciples came to him and said, "This is a deserted place, and the hour is now late; send the crowds away so that they may go into the villages and buy food for themselves." [16] Jesus said to them, "They need not go away; you give them something to eat." [17] They replied, "We have nothing here but five loaves and two fish." [18] And he said, "Bring them here to me." [19] Then he ordered the crowds to sit down on the grass. Taking the five loaves and the two fish, he looked up to heaven, and blessed and broke the loaves, and gave them to the disciples, and the disciples gave them to the crowds. [20] And all ate and were filled; and they took up what was left over of the broken pieces,

twelve baskets full. 21 And those who ate were about five thousand men, besides women and children.

Alone at Last

22 Immediately he made the disciples get into the boat and go on ahead to the other side, while he dismissed the crowds. 23 And after he had dismissed the crowds, he went up the mountain by himself to pray. When evening came, he was there alone, 24 but by this time the boat, battered by the waves, was far from the land, for the wind was against them. 25 And early in the morning he came walking toward them on the sea. 26 But when the disciples saw him walking on the sea, they were terrified, saying, "It is a ghost!" And they cried out in fear. 27 But immediately Jesus spoke to them and said, "Take heart, it is I; do not be afraid."

28 Peter answered him, "Lord, if it is you, command me to come to you on the water." 29 He said, "Come." So Peter got out of the boat, started walking on the water, and came toward Jesus. 30 But when he noticed the strong wind, he became frightened, and beginning to sink, he cried out, "Lord, save me!" 31 Jesus immediately reached out his hand and caught him, saying to him, "You of little faith, why did you doubt?" 32 When they got into the boat, the wind ceased. 33 And those in the boat worshiped him, saying, "Truly you are the Son of God."

The Crowds Return

34 When they had crossed over, they came to land at Gennesaret. 35 After the people of that place recognized him, they sent word throughout the region and brought all who were sick to him, 36 and begged him that they might touch even the fringe of his cloak; and all who touched it were healed.

10 minutes
Choose questions according to your interest and time.

1 Although Herod wants to put John to death (14:3–5), he is unhappy at the request of Herodias's daughter to have John beheaded (14:8–9). What might have caused his unhappiness?

2 In 14:16, what does Jesus really expect his disciples to do?

3 This reading contains accounts of two meals: Herod's (14:6–11) and Jesus' (14:15–21). How do the meals compare in terms of the values they express and the kinds of relationships the participants have with one another?

4 Why does Peter ask Jesus to call him out of the boat (14:28)?

5 What does Jesus mean by saying that Peter had "little faith" (14:31)?

6 If this reading represents a typical couple of days in Jesus' public life, what do you think life was like for the disciples who were with him?

A Guide to the Reading

If participants have not read this section already, read it aloud. Otherwise go on to "Questions for Application."

14:1–12. Who is Jesus? The question runs throughout this chapter. The residents of Nazareth, where he grew up, have just rejected the idea that there is anything very special about him (13:54–58). To them, Jesus appears to be just an ordinary man, their neighbor. Herod, in a confused way, at least recognizes that Jesus is extraordinary.

Herod had violated the Mosaic law by marrying his half brother's wife (Leviticus 18:16)—a violation that John the Baptist publicly condemned. Criticism from a popular preacher was a threat to the government, so Herod put John in prison.

Jesus and John knew each other. The two men may well have spent time together before Jesus began his own ministry (see 3:13–15). After Jesus' baptism, they continued to communicate (11:2–6). The news of John's murder would naturally be disturbing to Jesus—not only because of his friendship with John but also because, as Jesus knew, John's death foreshadowed what lay in store for him too. Apparently Jesus leaves the crowds and sails across the lake to be "by himself" in order to digest this bad news and pray.

14:13–21. Faced with a crowd of hungry people, Jesus gives his disciples an astonishing challenge: "You give them something to eat" (14:16). The disciples do not even have enough food for themselves (14:17). Perhaps equally astonishing to the disciples, Jesus seems about to give away what little dinner they have (14:18).

Jesus' multiplication of bread and fish demonstrates his creative power—and something more. Forms of the words *take, bless, break,* and *give* will occur again in Matthew's account of the Last Supper (26:26). Thus Matthew hints at a link between this hillside feast and Jesus' final meal. The miracle of the loaves and fish is an image of what will happen at the Last Supper—and in every later celebration of the Lord's Supper in the Church: God will provide inexhaustible nourishment for his people.

14:22–33. Jesus' afternoon of teaching, healing, and multiplying food has been a lengthy detour from his attempt to get some time alone. At the end of the day, perhaps out of an urgent desire to bring his grief and foreboding to the Father in prayer, he compels the disciples to embark without him (14:22). After a very long day, finally he is "alone" (14:23).

Only here and in Gethsemane (26:36–44) does Matthew show us Jesus engaged in private prayer. On both occasions Jesus prays in the shadow of death—first John's, then his own. At Gethsemane he will struggle to surrender himself to his Father's will. Has the struggle already begun here? The seriousness of Jesus' prayer is indicated by the circumstances: a storm comes up and rages across the lake, yet for hours he remains riveted to the mountain in prayer.

By walking across the lake, Jesus does what only the creator can do. God "alone stretched out the heavens and trampled the waves of the Sea" (Job 9:8). "Don't be afraid," Jesus tells the startled disciples. "It's *me*" (14:27). In one sense, Jesus is simply assuring them that the figure they are seeing is him, Jesus. Yet his manner of identifying himself echoes the way that God speaks about himself in the Old Testament. Literally Jesus says, "I am" (14:27), the same words that God used to reveal himself to Moses (Exodus 3:14). Jesus indicates that in seeing him, his disciples are encountering God.

Peter, frightened yet fascinated, asks Jesus to call him out onto the water with him. After making a good start, Peter (literally) "sees the wind"—an odd expression, but probably Matthew's way of saying that Peter stopped seeing Jesus. As soon as Peter takes his eyes off Jesus, he begins to sink. Quickly turning back to Jesus, Peter cries out the prayer that countless others have prayed: "Lord, save me!"

The episode points out that Jesus' presence will not save us from all storms. Rather, storms are where we may sometimes encounter him most directly. When we do, are we willing to get out of the boat and go to him?

14:34–36. People try to touch the hem of Jesus' garment (14:36). Like the cloaks of other Jewish men of the time, it probably had a colored fringe—a reminder to the wearer of belonging to God's people, Israel. Who is Jesus? He is a man from Nazareth, a first-century Palestinian Jew, a person of his particular place and culture. Yet he exercises divine powers: healing (14:14, 36), creating (14:19–21), mastering nature (14:25, 32). He speaks of himself in divine terms and accepts his disciples' worship (14:27, 33).

Questions for Application

40 minutes
Choose questions according to your interest and time.

1 Reread 14:17. Describe a time in your life when it seemed that God was asking you to do something for which you did not have the strength, training, or resources. How did you respond? What was the outcome?

2 Reread 14:17–20. When have you seen a small act of generosity make a big impact? What small act of generosity could you resolve to make?

3 Jesus sailed across a lake to find a quiet place to pray. How far out of your way do you go to create an opportunity to give God your full attention in prayer?

4 In what situation in your life do you feel like you are rowing against the wind and not making progress? What is the message of 14:24–33 for you?

5 Jesus' question to Peter—"Why did you doubt?" (14:31)—is a call to self-examination: "Think back over your experience, Peter. Identify where you went wrong. Correct the problem for the next occasion." Think of a situation in which you had doubts about God's presence or help. What did you do? What lesson can you learn from this experience?

6 For personal reflection: When we celebrate the Eucharist we come into contact with the same Jesus who presided over the miraculous meal on the hillside. Do you come to Mass expecting to encounter him, to hear his voice, to experience his healing power? What can you do to increase your expectation of these things?

Our daily reading of Scripture . . . is slow reading, leisurely reading, reading with attention to detail and nuance.

George Martin, *Reading Scripture as the Word of God*

Approach to Prayer

15 minutes
Use this approach—or create your own!

◆ Ask someone to read 14:15–21 aloud. Allow a time of silence for participants to identify an area of life in which God has called them to be of service to others. Invite them to name this area of service if they feel comfortable doing so. Then ask them to name one resource that they have for this service, such as "my time," "my desire to help," "my own experience of need," "my skill." Then pray the following prayer together:

Thank you, Lord, for calling us to serve you by serving our families, friends, and neighbors, by serving people who are strangers to us—people near and far, in all their various needs. Compared with the need, our resources are small and few, but we offer them to you, knowing that you can multiply what little we have. We offer ourselves to you, Lord. Guide us and do with us as you will.

Saints in the Making

A Multiplication of Tamales and Ham

This section is a supplement for individual reading.

One December in El Paso, Texas, a group of Christians studying the Bible together happened to read Luke 14:12–14, in which Jesus says that when you give a dinner, do not invite your friends or rich neighbors, but invite the poor and you will be repaid at the resurrection. They decided that on Christmas they would share their dinner with the poorest people they knew. So on Christmas Day they cooked some food, crossed the border into Juárez, Mexico, and drove to the city dump, where some people eked out a living by sorting trash.

"We brought food for 120 people," Fr. Rick Thomas, S.J., recalls. "About 250 to 300 showed up. We told the people that we didn't have enough for everyone but we would share what we had brought. They said, 'Let the children eat first.' Asking God's blessing, we began to eat. Somehow there was enough for everybody. Many who were there said that God had simply multiplied the tamales. The people got their food, and we sat down on the ground and had our little Christmas meal together. When the meal was over, they went back to work, sorting through the garbage. We took a stroll through the dump and visited some of the people."

One of the participants from El Paso, Frank Alarcon, said a little more about the multiplication of the food: "On the tailgate of my truck were two boneless hams. One lady kept cutting the ham until she tired, and then she handed the knife to someone else. The ham got smaller, but oh so slowly. Finally, everyone had a big piece of ham. Pockets were stuffed with food and children were carrying sacks away. On the way home, we had enough left to stop by and leave some at the orphanage. Every time I think about it I get goose bumps all over."

A miracle? Perhaps. But whatever happened to the food that day, something deeper happened to the people from El Paso. They began to work with their new acquaintances in Juárez. Since that Christmas, in 1971, their efforts have led to the development of a multifaceted outreach, Our Lady's Youth Center, which has grown to encompass a school, a daycare center, and medical, dental, and optical clinics. Today numerous volunteers are involved in the distribution of food and clothing, as well as in a children's meal program and a prison visitation program.

HALFWAY THERE

Questions to Begin

15 minutes
Use a question or two to get warmed up for the reading.

1 How good are you at predicting the weather?

2 When was the last time you lost your keys?

5 minutes
Read the passage aloud. Let individuals take turns reading paragraphs.

The Reading: Matthew 16

What Good Would a Sign Do?

[1] The Pharisees and Sadducees came, and to test Jesus they asked him to show them a sign from heaven. [2] He answered them, "When it is evening, you say, 'It will be fair weather, for the sky is red.' [3] And in the morning, 'It will be stormy today, for the sky is red and threatening.' You know how to interpret the appearance of the sky, but you cannot interpret the signs of the times. [4] An evil and adulterous generation asks for a sign, but no sign will be given to it except the sign of Jonah." Then he left them and went away.

Will They Ever Learn?

[5] When the disciples reached the other side, they had forgotten to bring any bread. [6] Jesus said to them, "Watch out, and beware of the yeast of the Pharisees and Sadducees." [7] They said to one another, "It is because we have brought no bread." [8] And becoming aware of it, Jesus said, "You of little faith, why are you talking about having no bread? [9] Do you still not perceive? Do you not remember the five loaves for the five thousand, and how many baskets you gathered? [10] Or the seven loaves for the four thousand, and how many baskets you gathered? [11] How could you fail to perceive that I was not speaking about bread? Beware of the yeast of the Pharisees and Sadducees!" [12] Then they understood that he had not told them to beware of the yeast of bread, but of the teaching of the Pharisees and Sadducees.

Now Do They Understand?

[13] Now when Jesus came into the district of Caesarea Philippi, he asked his disciples, "Who do people say that the Son of Man is?" [14] And they said, "Some say John the Baptist, but others Elijah, and still others Jeremiah or one of the prophets." [15] He said to them, "But who do you say that I am?" [16] Simon Peter answered, "You are the Messiah, the Son of the living God." [17] And Jesus answered him, "Blessed are you, Simon son of Jonah! For flesh and blood has not revealed this to you, but my Father in heaven. [18] And I tell you, you are Peter, and on this rock I will build my church, and the gates of

Hades will not prevail against it. [19] I will give you the keys of the kingdom of heaven, and whatever you bind on earth will be bound in heaven, and whatever you loose on earth will be loosed in heaven." [20] Then he sternly ordered the disciples not to tell anyone that he was the Messiah.

Are They Willing?

[21] From that time on, Jesus began to show his disciples that he must go to Jerusalem and undergo great suffering at the hands of the elders and chief priests and scribes, and be killed, and on the third day be raised. [22] And Peter took him aside and began to rebuke him, saying, "God forbid it, Lord! This must never happen to you." [23] But he turned and said to Peter, "Get behind me, Satan! You are a stumbling block to me; for you are setting your mind not on divine things but on human things."

[24] Then Jesus told his disciples, "If any want to become my followers, let them deny themselves and take up their cross and follow me. [25] For those who want to save their life will lose it, and those who lose their life for my sake will find it. [26] For what will it profit them if they gain the whole world but forfeit their life? Or what will they give in return for their life?

[27] "For the Son of Man is to come with his angels in the glory of his Father, and then he will repay everyone for what has been done. [28] Truly I tell you, there are some standing here who will not taste death before they see the Son of Man coming in his kingdom."

Questions for Careful Reading

10 minutes
Choose questions according to your interest and time.

1 Earlier Jesus told his disciples to take nothing with them on their missionary journeys (10:9–10). Yet the disciples seem to be in the habit of bringing supplies with them—at least, when they remember (14:17; 16:5). How would you explain this discrepancy?

2 What does Jesus seem to mean by the phrase "flesh and blood" in 16:17?

3 Why does Jesus wait until after the incident in 16:13–20 to speak to his disciples about his approaching death (16:21) and its implications for them (16:24–26)?

4 What might have been Jesus' reason for giving the instruction he does in 16:20?

5 Who is Peter concerned about in 16:22?

6 Jesus uses the word *want* twice in 16:24–25. What point is he trying to make?

A Guide to the Reading

If participants have not read this section already, read it aloud. Otherwise go on to "Questions for Application."

16:1–4. Jesus has now performed two miraculous multiplications of food (14:15–21; 15:32–38) and numerous healings. How sincere can the religious leaders' demand for a sign be? They ask for a sign from "heaven" (or in the "sky"—in Greek the two notions are expressed by the same word). Thus Jesus' answer is sarcastic: "You ask for a sign in the sky because you know so much about interpreting signs in the sky! Too bad you can't understand what is happening on the ground, right in front of you."

    16:5–12. The disciples have forgotten to bring along leftovers from Jesus' second miraculous feeding. Their failure to understand Jesus' warning is a case study in how preoccupation with our immediate problems (and lack of trust in God) can interfere with our hearing what God wishes to communicate to us.

    The Pharisees and the Sadducees are rival groups. They do, however, have something in common: a refusal to recognize Jesus for who he is. And who *is* Jesus? The question is about to receive a definitive answer.

    16:13–20. "You are the Messiah." Peter is the first person in Matthew's Gospel to express this recognition of Jesus. Scholar David Garland observes: "The Pharisees and the Sadducees demanded a sign from heaven and will receive nothing (16:1–4); Peter demanded nothing and receives a revelation from heaven." What is hidden from the wise and understanding is revealed to babes (11:25–27).

    Peter's recognition of Jesus as the supreme agent of God's purposes for the human race is a crucial milestone. The disciples have now reached the midpoint of the journey that began when Jesus called them to follow him and will reach its climax when he appears to them after his resurrection (4:18–22; 28:16–20).

    Peter has recognized Jesus' role in God's plan; now Jesus informs Peter of the role he is to play in this plan. In Greek, Peter's name is a form of a word meaning rock, cliff, bedrock. The corresponding word in Aramaic—the language that Jesus and the disciples spoke—means rocky crag ("Cephas"—see Galatians 1:18). Jesus means that Peter himself, not merely his statement of faith, is the rock on which he will build his community. Jesus is making a statement about Peter, just as Peter has made a statement about Jesus.

Peter's role in Jesus' community will be to hold the keys, like a household steward in charge of the rooms and buildings of his master's estate. Peter will be the authoritative interpreter of Jesus' teaching. After his resurrection, Jesus, continuing to be present with his followers, will teach and rule them through Peter and the other apostles (see 18:18–20; 28:18–20). Peter will interpret God's will as Jesus has revealed it so that people may know the path that leads into God's kingdom (7:13–14).

16:21–28. Having concluded the first phase of his training of his disciples, Jesus immediately turns the page and begins the next chapter of their instruction (16:21). Peter has recognized something important about Jesus, but his vision is blurred. In his mind's eye, Peter sees Jesus bringing some sort of political realm on earth. Jesus bursts this bubble by announcing his approaching death.

Perhaps Peter tries to dissuade Jesus from his plan out of concern for Jesus rather than concern for himself. If Peter is showing compassion, however, it is not the kind Jesus wants. Poor Peter: he goes from being bedrock to being a stumbling block without even passing Go. Peter, the foundation of Jesus' community, has become an obstacle to Jesus' accomplishing God's will. Jesus congratulated Peter because Peter was able to see him as God sees him, rather than from a merely human point of view (16:17). Now Jesus rebukes Peter for rejecting God's way of looking at things and for embracing a merely human viewpoint. The decisive factor in Peter's failure to grasp God's point of view is his inability to conceive of God acting through human suffering.

Jesus starkly characterizes Christian living as a walk with him from the place of sentencing to the place of execution (16:24). This, he affirms, is the only path to life, and traveling it is the only way to avoid eternal destruction (16:25–26).

The "coming" that Jesus says his disciples will witness (16:28) is probably not his final coming in judgment *to earth* but his coming in resurrection *to the Father* to share in his reign (compare with Daniel 7:13–14).

Questions for Application

40 minutes
Choose questions according to your interest and time.

1 What signs of God's presence in the world have been especially important for building your faith?

2 How is it possible for a person to see signs of God's presence and power—even miraculous signs—and yet remain unconvinced?

3 When have you failed to detect a sign of God's presence or guidance? What have you learned about interpreting "the signs of the times"?

4 Reread 16:5–12. When have you been so preoccupied with a problem that you failed to hear or understand what God was trying to communicate to you?

5 What has helped you believe that Jesus is the Son of God?

6 Who could you help to see and understand Jesus better? How could you help them?

7 What can help a person to realize that they are looking at life from a purely human perspective rather than seeing life from God's point of view? How can we grow in seeing things as God sees them?

8 Describe a person you know who is an example of what Jesus speaks about in 16:25. How did this person become willing to lose their life for the sake of God's kingdom and for the welfare of other people? How could you imitate this person more closely?

Holding the Bible in our hands is a lot easier than holding its message in our hearts. This assimilation takes a lifetime of conversion.

Steve Mueller, *The Seeker's Guide to Reading the Bible*

Approach to Prayer

15 minutes
Use this approach—or create your own!

◆ Ask someone to read 16:24–25 aloud. Pause for silent reflection. Then pray together this prayer by Adrienne von Speyr, a twentieth-century Swiss woman who was a physician and mystic.

Take, Lord, my whole life; take it, I ask you, just as it is now, with all that it is, with my strengths, my intentions and efforts, but also with everything that still pulls away from you, that I have set aside for myself; take all of that, too, together with the rest that I offer you. Take everything, so that all may be yours.

End with a Glory to the Father.

Saints in the Making

A Man Who Changed

This section is a supplement for individual reading.

When Jesus began to predict that he would soon suffer a painful death, his chief disciple, Peter, initially responded with alarm. Peter "took him aside and began to rebuke him, saying, 'God forbid it, Lord! This must never happen to you'" (16:22). Peter did not want Jesus to suffer—and did not want him to lead his disciples toward suffering. Later, after Jesus was arrested, Peter was so afraid of standing with Jesus that he publicly denied even knowing him (26:69–75).

Following Jesus' death and resurrection, however, Peter changed. The New Testament provides accounts of Peter that show him acting with boldness in the face of danger and hardship (Acts 4:1–13; 5:12–32). But the decisive evidence of Peter's newfound willingness to follow his master even into suffering lies beyond the reports in the New Testament.

There is no account of Peter's death in any writing from the first century. But around the year 96, Clement, a leader of the church in Rome, mentioned Peter's death in a letter to the church in Corinth. Clement refers to Peter as one who, "on account of wicked envy, endured not one or two but many sufferings, and, when he had borne witness in this way, went to the glorious place that he deserved." Clement does not describe Peter's death or say who was so envious of him. But his statement indicates that Peter died as a martyr.

Clement does not state that Peter died in Rome, but historians find clues in Clement's letter indicating that Peter died there, and there is no early Church tradition claiming that he died anywhere else. Probably he perished in the first great persecution of Christians, carried out by the emperor Nero in the year 64. A line in John's Gospel contains a hint that he died by crucifixion ("you will stretch out your hands"—John 21:18).

Peter did not establish the church in Rome. But his death there formed a profound bond between him and the Christian community in this city. Thus, over the centuries, as Christians grew in their understanding of the continuing role of Peter in the Church (see 16:17–19), it was the bishop of Rome who was seen as Peter's successor, authorized to exercise Peter's pastoral role in the whole Church.

How to Build a Community

Questions to Begin

15 minutes
Use a question or two to get warmed up for the reading.

1 When has something you needed come your way unexpectedly?

2 Describe a recent situation in which you had to ask someone to give you a little more time.

Opening the Bible

5 minutes
Read the passage aloud. Let individuals take turns reading
paragraphs.

The Reading: Matthew 17:24–27; 18:1–10, 19–35

Children of the King

24 When they reached Capernaum, the collectors of the temple tax
came to Peter and said, "Does your teacher not pay the temple tax?"
25 He said, "Yes, he does." And when he came home, Jesus spoke of it
first, asking, "What do you think, Simon? From whom do kings of
the earth take toll or tribute? From their children or from others?"
26 When Peter said, "From others," Jesus said to him, "Then the
children are free. 27 However, so that we do not give offense to them,
go to the sea and cast a hook; take the first fish that comes up; and
when you open its mouth, you will find a coin; take that and give it to
them for you and me."

True Greatness

18:1 At that time the disciples came to Jesus and asked, "Who is the
greatest in the kingdom of heaven?" 2 He called a child, whom he put
among them, 3 and said, "Truly I tell you, unless you change and
become like children, you will never enter the kingdom of heaven.
4 Whoever becomes humble like this child is the greatest in the
kingdom of heaven. 5 Whoever welcomes one such child in my name
welcomes me."

Stumbling Blocks

6 "If any of you put a stumbling block before one of these little ones
who believe in me, it would be better for you if a great millstone were
fastened around your neck and you were drowned in the depth of the
sea. 7 Woe to the world because of stumbling blocks! Occasions for
stumbling are bound to come, but woe to the one by whom the
stumbling block comes!
    8 "If your hand or your foot causes you to stumble, cut it off
and throw it away; it is better for you to enter life maimed or lame
than to have two hands or two feet and to be thrown into the eternal
fire. 9 And if your eye causes you to stumble, tear it out and throw it
away; it is better for you to enter life with one eye than to have two
eyes and to be thrown into the hell of fire.

¹⁰ "Take care that you do not despise one of these little ones; for, I tell you, in heaven their angels continually see the face of my Father in heaven. . . ."

Jesus' Presence

¹⁹ "Again, truly I tell you, if two of you agree on earth about anything you ask, it will be done for you by my Father in heaven. ²⁰ For where two or three are gathered in my name, I am there among them."

Forgiveness

²¹ Then Peter came and said to him, "Lord, if another member of the church[a] sins against me, how often should I forgive? As many as seven times?" ²² Jesus said to him, "Not seven times, but, I tell you, seventy-seven times.

²³ "For this reason the kingdom of heaven may be compared to a king who wished to settle accounts with his slaves. ²⁴ When he began the reckoning, one who owed him ten thousand talents was brought to him; ²⁵ and, as he could not pay, his lord ordered him to be sold, together with his wife and children and all his possessions, and payment to be made. ²⁶ So the slave fell on his knees before him, saying, 'Have patience with me, and I will pay you everything.' ²⁷ And out of pity for him, the lord of that slave released him and forgave him the debt. ²⁸ But that same slave, as he went out, came upon one of his fellow slaves who owed him a hundred denarii; and seizing him by the throat, he said, 'Pay what you owe.' ²⁹ Then his fellow slave fell down and pleaded with him, 'Have patience with me, and I will pay you.' ³⁰ But he refused; then he went and threw him into prison until he would pay the debt. ³¹ When his fellow slaves saw what had happened, they were greatly distressed, and they went and reported to their lord all that had taken place. ³² Then his lord summoned him and said to him, 'You wicked slave! I forgave you all that debt because you pleaded with me. ³³ Should you not have had mercy on your fellow slave, as I had mercy on you?' ³⁴ And in anger his lord handed him over to be tortured until he would pay his entire debt. ³⁵ So my heavenly Father will also do to every one of you, if you do not forgive your brother or sister from your heart."

[a] Greek *if my brother*

Questions for Careful Reading

10 minutes
Choose questions according to your interest and time.

1 Why would Peter give the tax collectors the answer he does in 17:25?

2 In Scripture, the number seven sometimes symbolizes completeness. If that symbolism is operative in 18:21–22, what might seventy-seven represent?

3 Judging from chapter 18, what kinds of people does Jesus expect will belong to his Church?

4 Here's a special challenge question for extra credit. Remember story problems in grade school math? Try this one. If one talent of silver was worth ten thousand denarii, and one denarius was the minimum wage for a day's work, how many workdays would be required to pay off a debt of ten thousand talents (18:24)? Using fifty dollars as an approximation of a day's pay at the current minimum wage, what would be the dollar value of the debt today?

A Guide to the Reading

If participants have not read this section already, read it aloud. Otherwise go on to "Questions for Application."

17:24–27. The disciples have been trekking around Galilee with Jesus for some time. Now Jesus has paused, and the group is taking a little R and R at Capernaum, Peter's hometown. We may wonder how relaxing the return home is for Peter, who hasn't fixed a leaky faucet in weeks. The mundane demands of life quickly reassert themselves in the person of some tax collectors who appear at the door.

With his deep respect for the Mosaic law (5:17–20), Jesus does not oppose supporting the temple. He does, however, oppose supporting it through a tax, because taxation treats those who pay it as though they are not God's children. A central element of Jesus' teaching is that God wishes us to relate to him as our Father ("Our Father in heaven . . ."—6:9–13).

This episode is unique in conveying a sense of the master-disciple friendship between Jesus and Peter. I picture Jesus putting his arm around Peter's shoulders and saying, "Peter, let's take care of this problem together." Wouldn't we all like to have that kind of relationship with Jesus in many situations in our lives? Perhaps Matthew included the story in his Gospel to assure us that we *can.*

18:1–5. Children are weak and dependent. In Jesus' day, they were socially insignificant. If they played any role at all, it was to serve (a form of the Greek word for child used here also means servant). When he talks of becoming humble, Jesus does not mean developing a poor self-image but seeing ourselves as dependent on God and assigned to serve others. How can we become like children? That's easy: by serving children (18:5)—and others who are weak, dependent, and regarded as less valuable. (Jesus is staying at Peter's house. Is the child in this episode Peter's?)

18:6–10. Jesus was willing to pay the tax to avoid leading others into sin by seeming to neglect the needs of the temple. Now he returns to the subject of leading others into sin. The Greek term translated "give offense" in 17:27 is used also in 18:6 (translated "put a stumbling block") and in 18:8–9 ("causes you to stumble").

Jesus gives a stern warning about giving bad example to others (18:7). (Did he illustrate his teaching by gesturing toward the lake of Galilee? It was just a minute's walk from Peter's house.)

Jesus' point is that we are responsible for one another. This might lead to a belief that we can blame others for our sins, but Jesus immediately rules that out, giving an equally stern warning about letting our own desires lead us into sin (18:8–9). Each of us is responsible for our own behavior. If we feel tempted to do wrong, Jesus says, we should take action against that temptation. Blaming our sins on other people, or even on our own impulses and weaknesses, will not be accepted when we appear in the heavenly court.

18:19–20. Jesus' promise of his presence is at the center of his instructions about living as his community. This suggests that praying together is the key to being able to respond to his challenging instructions.

18:21–35. St. John Chrysostom thought that Peter supposed himself to be the author of a great saying when he proposed forgiveness seven times, since seven often symbolizes completeness. Peter's question means "Do you expect me to always forgive my brothers and sisters?" Jesus' answer amounts to saying, "Absolutely!"

The annual tax income of the region governed by Herod (14:1) was only two hundred talents. No servant in the ancient world could ever have gotten himself into a debt as gigantic as the one in the parable—nor could any servant ever have gotten himself out of such a debt. Nevertheless, as Fr. George Montague, a New Testament scholar, observes, "the servant does what every pressed debtor does: he does not ask to be released from the debt but 'just give me time.'" Selling the servant and his family would yield only a talent or two—leaving 9,998 talents still owed.

"You wicked slave!" Although the king did not get angry at the slave for running up the gargantuan debt, he becomes furious with him for failing to have mercy on a fellow servant. The servant has failed to show a fellow servant even a tiny fraction of the mercy that he has just experienced himself. The king's command to have the servant tortured is not a punishment (18:34). Torturing a debtor was a way of persuading the person's family and friends to purchase their freedom by helping to pay off the debt.

Questions for Application

40 minutes
Choose questions according to your interest and time.

1 What does it mean to have God as one's Father? What have you learned about relating to God as your Father?

2 How would you distinguish authentic attempts to be humble and childlike from false ones?

3 How can a person grow in being genuinely humble? What obstacles keep you from growing in humility? How could you grow in humility?

4 When is it especially difficult to forgive? What can help a person to forgive others?

5   Jesus speaks of humbling ourselves (18:1–5) and forgiving (18:21–35). What connection is there between these two ways of relating to other people?

6   For personal reflection: Is there anything in how you speak or in the things you do that might provide someone else with justification or encouragement for doing something self-destructive or wrong? How should you change your behavior?

7   Also for personal reflection: Who do you need to forgive? How should you show your forgiveness?

Exercise your mind: feed it daily with Holy Scripture.

St. Jerome

Approach to Prayer

15 minutes
Use this approach—or create your own!

◆ Let someone read aloud 18:35 and this excerpt from the *Catechism of the Catholic Church:*

It is there . . . "in the depths of the *heart,*" that everything is bound and loosed. It is not in our power not to feel or to forget an offense; but the heart that offers itself to the Holy Spirit turns injury into compassion and purifies the memory in transforming the hurt into intercession.

Then pray this prayer together a few times, each time filling in the blank with the references listed below—or with others, as you may wish.

Lord, show your mercy to_____.
May they know your love and be freed from every obstacle to your presence. Father, forgive us our trespasses as we forgive those who trespass against us.

. . . our parents, our brothers and sisters, and the older and younger members of our families . . . our classmates . . . people we have worked with . . . all who have injured us . . .

End with an Our Father.

A Living Tradition

Angel Guardians

This section is a supplement for individual reading.

J esus' statement that "in heaven their angels continually see the face of my Father in heaven" (18:10) has led the Church to be confident that "from its beginning until death, human life is surrounded by the watchful care and intercession" of angels (*Catechism of the Catholic Church*, section 336).

On Matthew 18:10, St. Jerome, a fourth-century biblical scholar, wrote: "Human beings have such a great dignity that each one, from the moment of birth, has a guardian angel assigned to him or her."

St. Thomas Aquinas, a great theologian of the thirteenth century, agreed with Jerome. While at least one early Church teacher, named Origen, had speculated that individuals receive a guardian angel at baptism, Thomas argued that each human being is appointed an angel guardian as he or she comes into the world. Thomas wrote:

Man while in this state of life is, as it were, on a road by which he should journey towards heaven. On this road man is threatened by many dangers both from within and from without, according to Psalm 142:3: "In the path where I walk they have hidden a trap for me." And therefore as guardians are appointed for men who have to pass by an unsafe road, so an angel guardian is assigned to each man as long as he is a wayfarer. When, however, he arrives at the end of life he no longer has a guardian angel; but in the kingdom he will have an angel to reign with him.

According to Thomas, angels do not force us to act or think in a certain way. They do, however, have the ability to strengthen our minds so that we can perceive the truth. And they can communicate God's wisdom to us so that we may better understand what we should believe and do. Angels, Thomas taught, have the power to help us see the goodness of God's will for us and to stir up our desire to follow it. He added that while the principal purpose of angel guardianship is to guide us to our heavenly home, "nevertheless it has many other effects . . . for instance, to ward off the demons and to prevent both bodily and spiritual harm."

COMMANDMENTS AND INVITATIONS

Questions to Begin

15 minutes
Use a question or two to get warmed up for the reading.

1 If you could ask Jesus a difficult question, what would it be?

2 Name one very happy married couple you have known. Identify one reason why they seemed so happy.

Opening the Bible

5 minutes
Read the passage aloud. Let individuals take turns reading paragraphs.

The Reading: Matthew 19:1–26

About Marriage and Divorce

¹ When Jesus had finished saying these things, he left Galilee and went to the region of Judea beyond the Jordan. ² Large crowds followed him, and he cured them there.

³ Some Pharisees came to him, and to test him they asked, "Is it lawful for a man to divorce his wife for any cause?" ⁴ He answered, "Have you not read that the one who made them at the beginning 'made them male and female,' ⁵ and said, 'For this reason a man shall leave his father and mother and be joined to his wife, and the two shall become one flesh'? ⁶ So they are no longer two, but one flesh. Therefore what God has joined together, let no one separate." ⁷ They said to him, "Why then did Moses command us to give a certificate of dismissal and to divorce her?" ⁸ He said to them, "It was because you were so hard-hearted that Moses allowed you to divorce your wives, but from the beginning it was not so. ⁹ And I say to you, whoever divorces his wife, except for unchastity, and marries another commits adultery."

About Remaining Unmarried

¹⁰ His disciples said to him, "If such is the case of a man with his wife, it is better not to marry." ¹¹ But he said to them, "Not everyone can accept this teaching, but only those to whom it is given. ¹² For there are eunuchs who have been so from birth, and there are eunuchs who have been made eunuchs by others, and there are eunuchs who have made themselves eunuchs for the sake of the kingdom of heaven. Let anyone accept this who can."

About Children

¹³ Then little children were being brought to him in order that he might lay his hands on them and pray. The disciples spoke sternly to those who brought them; ¹⁴ but Jesus said, "Let the little children come to me, and do not stop them; for it is to such as these that the kingdom of heaven belongs." ¹⁵ And he laid his hands on them and went on his way.

About Wealth

16 Then someone came to him and said, "Teacher, what good deed must I do to have eternal life?" 17 And he said to him, "Why do you ask me about what is good? There is only one who is good. If you wish to enter into life, keep the commandments." 18 He said to him, "Which ones?" And Jesus said, "You shall not murder; You shall not commit adultery; You shall not steal; You shall not bear false witness; 19 Honor your father and mother; also, You shall love your neighbor as yourself." 20 The young man said to him, "I have kept all these; what do I still lack?" 21 Jesus said to him, "If you wish to be perfect, go, sell your possessions, and give the money to the poor, and you will have treasure in heaven; then come, follow me." 22 When the young man heard this word, he went away grieving, for he had many possessions.

23 Then Jesus said to his disciples, "Truly I tell you, it will be hard for a rich person to enter the kingdom of heaven. 24 Again I tell you, it is easier for a camel to go through the eye of a needle than for someone who is rich to enter the kingdom of God." 25 When the disciples heard this, they were greatly astounded and said, "Then who can be saved?" 26 But Jesus looked at them and said, "For mortals it is impossible, but for God all things are possible."

Questions for Careful Reading

10 minutes
Choose questions according to your interest and time.

1 What does Jesus mean by *hard-heartedness* (19:8)? What effect can it have on a marriage?

2 Jesus says that a second marriage after divorce is "adultery." Why?

3 What is the disciples' attitude toward marriage (19:10)? How does it compare with Jesus' attitude?

4 Compare the encounters with children in 18:1–5 (in last week's reading; page 45) and 19:13. How good are Jesus' disciples at remembering their master's instructions?

5 The young man asserts that he has kept all the commandments (19:20). Does Jesus agree or disagree?

6 Jesus tells the man to sell his possessions and give the proceeds to the poor (19:21). What is the relationship between doing this and carrying out the last of the commands that Jesus mentions in 19:18–19?

A Guide to the Reading

If participants have not read this section already, read it aloud. Otherwise go on to "Questions for Application."

19:1–9. The Old Testament contains a regulation forbidding a husband who divorced his wife to remarry her if she has subsequently married and been divorced from another man (Deuteronomy 24:1–4). This regulation assumes that divorces will occur and stipulates that the divorcing husband should write out a certificate of dismissal for his wife. On the basis of this stipulation, divorce was freely practiced among Jews in first-century Palestine.

Jesus has already spoken against divorce (5:31–32). Knowing this, the Pharisees see an opportunity to make a triple play against him. They ask him whether there is *any* ground for divorce. If, as expected, he answers no, he will discredit himself by publicly contradicting the law of Moses, which permits divorce. He will also alienate married men who value their easy access to divorce. And he will get himself into trouble with the government, since forbidding divorce could be interpreted as a criticism of Herod and Herodias, who have divorced their spouses to marry each other. We saw earlier what could happen to a person for openly criticizing Herod's marital escapades (14:3–11).

Jesus reaches behind Moses' rule about divorce and cites God's original plan for marriage (19:4–6; Genesis 1:27; 2:23–24). Jesus implies that now that God's kingdom is arriving (4:17), God's original plan will be fulfilled. When the Pharisees object that Moses gave a *command* regarding divorce, Jesus points out that Moses gave only *permission* for it. By removing this permission for divorce, Jesus implies that he brings the solution to the hardness of heart that causes it.

Jesus mentions a condition that creates an exception to his no-divorce approach: "unchastity" by the wife. (Within the patriarchal culture of the first century, the Pharisees and Jesus consider the issue of divorce from the husband's point of view. But Jesus draws forth a principle that applies equally to men and women. This equality is made clearer in Mark 10:10–12.) What is this "unchastity"? It may refer to marrying someone related too closely by blood according to the Mosaic law (Leviticus 18:16–18). For any of Matthew's readers from a gentile background who had entered into such marriages before becoming Christians, Jesus' words would mean that they could now separate, since their marriages were not legitimate. "Unchastity" may also refer to sexual wrongdoing, such as adultery. Jewish men of the time might have felt that they were not only permitted but even obliged to separate from a wife who violated the marriage by such "unchastity." This seems to have been what Joseph was thinking, for example, when he discovered that Mary, his betrothed, had become pregnant without him (1:19). It took the visit of an angel to persuade Joseph to abandon his plan to divorce her (1:20–24).

In such cases of "unchastity," is the husband free to remarry? Simply from the wording of verse 9, the answer may not be absolutely clear. But the definitive interpretation of the Church, from early times, has ruled out this possibility (see the *Catechism of the Catholic Church,* sections 2382–2386).

The religious leaders have failed to provoke Jesus into contradicting a Mosaic instruction. Jesus has grounded his interpretation of one Torah passage (in Deuteronomy) in another passage in the Torah (in Genesis). By removing the permission for divorce, Jesus has not overturned God's law regarding marriage any more than canceling a tax exemption nullifies the tax code of which it is a part.

19:10–12. At first, it might seem that Jesus agrees with the apostles' statement that if divorce is impossible, it is better to remain single. But that would reflect a negative attitude toward marriage, and Jesus has just said that God regards marriage as such a great good that he forbids anyone from disrupting it (19:6). God *likes* marriage; it is a wonderful part of his design for human beings. Jesus, then, agrees with the disciples only partially. Refraining from marriage can be better than marrying, but not for the reason the disciples are thinking of. Marriage is good, but in the case of some people, God's purpose is best achieved by their remaining single.

In speaking of teaching that not everyone can "accept," Jesus does not seem to be referring back to his teaching on divorce. *That* teaching is not difficult to understand, and he presents it as compelling for all. The teaching that "not everyone can accept" refers to celibacy for God's kingdom—remaining single in order to be as free as possible to follow Jesus wherever he might lead. Significantly, Jesus presents his recommendation of celibacy in the context of his teaching about marriage. The high value that Jesus has just put on marriage shows that his recommendation of celibacy does not arise from any depreciation of marriage.

19:13–15. St. John Chrysostom explains that the disciples think that Jesus is too important to be wasting his time with children, who lack social standing. There is an element of self-interest in their shooing the children away. Since they gain respect when their master gains respect, they do not want him to lose prestige by acting in an undignified manner. But Jesus shows how greatly he values those whom society does not.

19:16–30. Jesus treats the commandments as basic principles for his disciples to follow (19:17). Does he also expect all his followers to relinquish all their possessions (19:21)? There is no simple answer.

One consideration is that, in the circumstances of the time, Jesus' call to the young man is a call to justice. Unlike modern economies, ancient economies were able to grow only very slowly. In a static economy, one person could become rich only by making someone else poor. A rich person's accumulation of wealth directly represented resources taken away from others (compare with James 5:1–6). In this situation, Jesus' call to the young man to distribute his possessions to the poor is a call to give back what rightfully belongs to them. To the degree that Jesus' call to the young man is a call to justice, it remains a call to all his followers. Jesus' command to live justly, in a way that does not deprive others of what they need, does not mandate an identical lifestyle for all his disciples in every economic and social situation. But even in a world of economic growth, there is economic exploitation. Those of us who live in affluent nations benefit from the labor of countless people in poorer countries, many of them children, who work long hours in unhealthy conditions for woefully inadequate compensation to provide the materials and products that we enjoy. Thus we present-day disciples of Jesus must also confront the issue of justice that Jesus raises here with the young man.

Some have argued that in this episode Jesus is establishing a community with two tiers—some members following the commandments (19:17–19) and becoming "good," others following Jesus' further advice (19:21) and becoming "perfect." But in the Bible, "good" and "perfect" do not denote two different grades of virtue. When Jesus suggests that the man relinquish all and become his disciple in order to become "perfect," he is not offering him an optional fast track to eternal life. Jesus summons *all* his disciples to become "perfect" (5:48).

Furthermore, Jesus says of the rich that it is *impossible* for them to enter the kingdom of heaven (19:23–26). Thus it could hardly have been merely optional for the rich man to divest himself of his wealth. Jesus implies that if he does not do so, he will not enter the kingdom.

Yet there seems to be a unique quality to Jesus' invitation to this man to give up everything. Perhaps Jesus was acting on a pastoral insight into the man's character. Was this man especially vulnerable to the suffocating effects of earthly cares (see 13:22)?

Clearly Jesus did not require all those who believed in him to sell all their belongings and distribute them to the poor. Some of those who believed in him remained in their houses and kept their jobs (8:5–13, 14; 9:2–7). He envisaged disciples who would stay at home as well as disciples who would go out on mission (10:40–42).

So where does that leave us? New Testament scholar Ulrich Luz suggests that "Matthew probably understands the demand to give up one's possessions neither as a law for everyone nor as advice for a few but as an appeal to all to go this way as far as possible." Jesus' call to serve one's neighbor has no limit. It extends even to loving one's enemy (5:43–48). Here Jesus challenges the young man to give away his wealth as a radical expression of love. "To become perfect is to go beyond what is normal and customary," Luz remarks. "It is to embark on a way that reflects something of Jesus' own radical life."

In each of the episodes in this reading, the disciples take a different view from that of Jesus. They find his teaching as astounding as his miracles. It almost seems as though they need a miracle of enlightenment to enable them to accept Jesus' teaching and become people of faithfulness, humility, and love. Where might this miracle come from? The clue lies in Jesus' invitation to the rich young man: "Come, follow me."

Questions for Application

40 minutes
Choose questions according to your interest and time.

1 What married couple has been an example to you of Christian marriage? What could other couples learn from them? What could single people learn from them?

2 What are the most important qualities for a husband and a wife to cultivate in their relationship with each other?

3 How can Christians support married couples in their marriages? What more could your parish do to offer support? What contribution could you make?

4 What, specifically, do Jesus' words in 19:14 mean for you?

5 Why is wealth an obstacle to entering God's kingdom?

6 What kinds of things might a person have to leave behind in order to follow Jesus freely? What have you left behind in order to live as his follower?

7 What kind of response is Jesus seeking from you in 19:21?

8 Look back at incidents in which Jesus' disciples found his approach surprising, unexpected, puzzling, or even offensive (14:16–17; 16:5–12, 21–23; 17:24–27) and consider also such incidents in this week's reading (19:10–12, 13–14, 23–26). On what kinds of issues did the disciples have difficulty understanding Jesus? How did Jesus deal with his disciples' frequent failures to share his outlook? What impression of Jesus does this give you?

At some time during the group's study . . . it should become obvious that the search for biblical beauty, truth, and goodness is unending. As discovery leads to discovery, it surely will occur to the group that a definitive interpretation is extremely elusive.

Eugene LaVerdiere, S.S.S., "Bible Study: Sowing the Seed," *Church*

Approach to Prayer

15 minutes
Use this approach—or create your own!

◆ Pray some of Psalm 119, which expresses a longing to come close to the Lord through knowing and doing his will. A Christian praying this psalm may use the psalmist's references to obeying God's "precepts," "statutes," and "decrees" as a way of expressing a desire to respond to Jesus' calls and invitations to leave things behind and follow him. Suggested sections for group prayer: verses 1 through 8, verses 9 through 16, and verses 57 through 64. If all participants have the same translation of the Bible, you can pray the sections of the psalm in unison. If not, take turns reading individual verses from your particular translations.

A Living Tradition

An Invitation to Everyone

This section is a supplement for individual reading.

H ere are some comments by Pope John Paul II on Jesus' conversation with the rich young man, from his encyclical *The Splendor of Truth,* sections 7–19.

"Teacher, what good deed must I do to have eternal life?" The question is not so much about rules to be followed, but about the full meaning of life. . . . This question is ultimately an appeal to the absolute Good which attracts us and beckons us; it is the echo of a call from God who is the origin and goal of man's life.

"There is only one who is good." The "Good Teacher" points out to him . . . that the answer to the question . . . can only be found by turning one's mind and heart to the "One" who is good. . . . Only God can answer the question about what is good, because he is the Good itself. . . . God alone is worthy of being loved "with all one's heart. . . ." He is the source of man's happiness.

"If you wish to enter into life, keep the commandments." God's commandments show man the path of life.

"Which ones?" . . . "You shall not murder . . . commit adultery . . . bear false witness . . ." These negative precepts express . . . the ever urgent need to protect human life, the communion of persons in marriage, private property, truthfulness and people's good name. The commandments thus represent the basic condition for love of neighbor.

"What do I still lack?" Even though he has followed the moral ideal seriously and generously from childhood, the rich young man knows that he is still far from the goal: before the person of Jesus he realizes that he is still lacking something.

"If you wish to be perfect, go, sell your possessions, and give the money to the poor . . ." The invitation . . . and the promise "you will have treasure in heaven," are meant for everyone, because they bring out the full meaning of the commandment of love for neighbor.

"Come, follow me." Every believer is called to be a follower of Christ. . . . This is not a matter only of disposing oneself to hear a teaching and obediently accepting a commandment. . . . It involves holding fast to the very person of Jesus, partaking of his life . . . , sharing in his free and loving obedience to the will of the Father.

HAVE MERCY ON US, LORD!

Questions to Begin

15 minutes
Use a question or two to get warmed up for the reading.

1 What was your longest day of work? Did you feel a sense of accomplishment at the end of it or were you just glad to get the day over with?

2 Have you ever worked on a farm? If not, what is the closest you have ever come to doing farm-type work?

Opening the Bible

5 minutes
Read the passage aloud. Let individuals take turns reading
paragraphs.

The Reading: Matthew 19:27–20:34

What Reward Will We Get?

27 Peter said . . . , "Look, we have left everything and followed you.
What then will we have?" 28 Jesus said to them, "Truly I tell you,
at the renewal of all things, when the Son of Man is seated on the
throne of his glory, you who have followed me will also sit on twelve
thrones, judging the twelve tribes of Israel. 29 And everyone who
has left houses or brothers or sisters or father or mother or children
or fields, for my name's sake, will receive a hundredfold, and will
inherit eternal life. 30 But many who are first will be last, and the last
will be first.

20:1 "For the kingdom of heaven is like a landowner who went
out early in the morning to hire laborers for his vineyard. 2 After
agreeing with the laborers for the usual daily wage, he sent them into
his vineyard. 3 When he went out about nine o'clock, he saw others
standing idle in the marketplace; 4 and he said to them, 'You also go
into the vineyard, and I will pay you whatever is right.' So they went.
5 When he went out again about noon and about three o'clock, he did
the same. 6 And about five o'clock he went out and found others
standing around; and he said to them, 'Why are you standing here
idle all day?' 7 They said to him, 'Because no one has hired us.' He
said to them, 'You also go into the vineyard.' 8 When evening came,
the owner of the vineyard said to his manager, 'Call the laborers and
give them their pay, beginning with the last and then going to the
first.' 9 When those hired about five o'clock came, each of them
received the usual daily wage. 10 Now when the first came, they
thought they would receive more; but each of them also received the
usual daily wage. 11 And when they received it, they grumbled against
the landowner, 12 saying, 'These last worked only one hour, and you
have made them equal to us who have borne the burden of the day
and the scorching heat.' 13 But he replied to one of them, 'Friend, I
am doing you no wrong; did you not agree with me for the usual
daily wage? 14 Take what belongs to you and go; I choose to give to
this last the same as I give to you. 15 Am I not allowed to do what I
choose with what belongs to me? Or are you envious because I am
generous?' 16 So the last will be first, and the first will be last."

Slow Learners

17 While Jesus was going up to Jerusalem, he took the twelve disciples aside by themselves, and said to them on the way, 18 "See, we are going up to Jerusalem, and the Son of Man will be handed over to the chief priests and scribes, and they will condemn him to death; 19 then they will hand him over to the Gentiles to be mocked and flogged and crucified; and on the third day he will be raised."

20 Then the mother of the sons of Zebedee came to him with her sons, and kneeling before him, she asked a favor of him. 21 And he said to her, "What do you want?" She said to him, "Declare that these two sons of mine will sit, one at your right hand and one at your left, in your kingdom." 22 But Jesus answered, "You do not know what you are asking. Are you able to drink the cup that I am about to drink?" They said to him, "We are able." 23 He said to them, "You will indeed drink my cup, but to sit at my right hand and at my left, this is not mine to grant, but it is for those for whom it has been prepared by my Father."

24 When the ten heard it, they were angry with the two brothers. 25 But Jesus called them to him and said, "You know that the rulers of the Gentiles lord it over them, and their great ones are tyrants over them. 26 It will not be so among you; but whoever wishes to be great among you must be your servant, 27 and whoever wishes to be first among you must be your slave; 28 just as the Son of Man came not to be served but to serve, and to give his life a ransom for many."

Healing and Discipleship

29 As they were leaving Jericho, a large crowd followed him. 30 There were two blind men sitting by the roadside. When they heard that Jesus was passing by, they shouted, "Lord, have mercy on us, Son of David!" 31 The crowd sternly ordered them to be quiet; but they shouted even more loudly, "Have mercy on us, Lord, Son of David!" 32 Jesus stood still and called them, saying, "What do you want me to do for you?" 33 They said to him, "Lord, let our eyes be opened." 34 Moved with compassion, Jesus touched their eyes. Immediately they regained their sight and followed him.

10 minutes
Choose questions according to your interest and time.

1 Jesus' statement in 19:28–29 and his parable of the vineyard workers (20:1–16) are both answers to Peter's question in 19:27. In what way do these two answers balance each other out?

2 The statements Jesus makes in 19:30 and 20:16 form a kind of frame around the parable of the vineyard workers. In what way are the two statements similar? In what way are they different? How do they relate to the message of the parable? (There is no easy answer to this question, but Matthew presents the situation for our consideration.)

3 Jesus' announcement of his approaching death in 20:17–19 is his third such statement to his disciples (16:21; 17:22–23). Why does he keep repeating it?

4 What do 18:1 and 20:20–24 suggest about the disciples' way of relating to one another? What kind of change would Jesus like to see in their relationships with one another?

A Guide to the Reading

If participants have not read this section already, read it aloud. Otherwise go on to "Questions for Application."

19:27–20:16. Peter asks Jesus about the reward for leaving all to follow him, and Jesus gives him a two-part answer. The first part is immensely comforting: God will reward our efforts to follow his Son with extravagant generosity (19:28–29). The second part of Jesus' answer (20:1–16), however, may disturb our comfort. Earlier Jesus told a parable that appealed to our sense of fair play to explain how God relates to us (18:23–35). The parable that Jesus now tells violates our sense of fair play.

The story raises some questions that probably can't be answered. Why did the vineyard owner go repeatedly to the town square for laborers? Didn't he plan out his hiring? When he went back again in the late afternoon, he seemed to know that those who were unemployed had been so all day (20:6)—so why didn't he hire them earlier? The owner's approach to payment (20:8) ensured that the workers hired first would see what was paid to those hired last. Was he trying to provoke the early workers? And above all, why did he pay as he did? Granted, he was generous: he paid the later workers a full day's wage out of concern for their welfare. Paying them less would have given them less than they needed to feed their families. But if he was so generous, why didn't he pay the early workers more?

Some have suggested that the point of the parable is to overturn the whole idea of looking for a reward for serving God; it teaches that God's reward is pure gift, not a matter of just payment. Yet alongside the elements of generosity and gift are elements of justice and payment: the hiring for a wage, the agreement on payment, the performance of services agreed upon, the payment of wages. (On the subject of merit and eternal reward, see the *Catechism of the Catholic Church,* sections 2006–2011.)

The early laborers are not unhappy that the late laborers get a full day's pay. They do not lack solidarity with their coworkers. They expect, however, to receive more. They think they should get a bonus. They do not object to the owner's generosity to others; they object to his failure to show commensurate generosity to themselves. "You ought to be as generous with us as you were with them," they say. This claim the owner absolutely rejects.

The parable teaches that God is both just and generous. And he is free. He is free to go beyond mere justice, and free to decide how far beyond justice he will go with each person. With God, no one receives less than they deserve. But some receive far more. Indeed, don't we all?

20:17–28. Jesus again predicts his death. This is the first time he speaks specifically of being "crucified" (compare with 16:21 and 17:22–23). Despite his stark prediction, as he approaches Jerusalem his disciples think that he is about to make his move and seize political control. They assume that he will establish some sort of heavenly realm on earth, in which positions of authority and preeminence will be filled by loyal followers.

In a sense, Jesus' words here are a third answer to Peter's question about rewards. "If you're looking for special earthly honors and powers," he says, "you're looking in the wrong direction. Being my follower means imitating me. But I am not looking for recognition and power; I am looking to serve." Jesus' particular service involves abandoning all self-concern and submitting to a painful death for the sake of others.

20:29–34. Jesus has spoken difficult words about marriage and celibacy; about humbling oneself and assuming a posture of service to other people; about leaving behind security, comforts, and familiar people; about forgiving others and welcoming God's generosity toward them. He has laid out a program for personal change that requires a healing of the way one looks at oneself and others. His restoration of sight to two men in Jericho demonstrates that he himself is the source of this healing.

These two men are the last to become Jesus' disciples in Matthew's Gospel. By joining Jesus at the very end of his traveling ministry, they are like the vineyard workers in the parable who are hired at the eleventh hour. They are also the only male disciples in the Gospel to receive a physical healing from Jesus. Thus they give the other disciples a golden opportunity to put the message of the parable into practice.

The last word in our reading is of Jesus' "compassion" (20:34). We have ended our reading of Matthew's Gospel at the point where we began (9:36).

Questions for Application

40 minutes
Choose questions according to your interest and time.

1 Jesus speaks about rewards in "the renewal of all things" at the end of time (19:28–29). What benefits in this *present* world might a person experience from leaving things behind in order to follow Jesus?

2 Are the early workers envious of the later workers (20:15)? What is envy? Where does it come from? What can be done to overcome it?

3 Is the vineyard owner in the parable unfair? How does this parable challenge you to change your thinking about God?

4 Does the mother of James and John seek what is good or not? Why?

5 When have you observed someone who exemplified the attitude that Jesus recommends in 20:26–27? What particular action could you take to become more like this person?

6 Jesus' statement at the end of 20:28 implies that there is no limit to his willingness to serve others. Are there limits to the extent to which a person should seek to serve others? What limits do you set on your willingness to serve others?

7 What kind of service is Jesus calling you to as his follower in the world? How might you free yourself from other things in order to devote yourself more to this service?

As the reader matures in the life of the Spirit, there grows also his or her capacity to understand the realities of which the Bible speaks.

Pontifical Biblical Commission, *The Interpretation of the Bible in the Church*

Approach to Prayer

15 minutes
Use this approach—or create your own!

◆ Let one participant read aloud this excerpt from the Gospel (20:30–32):

When they heard that Jesus was passing by, they shouted, "Lord, have mercy on us, Son of David!" The crowd sternly ordered them to be quiet; but they shouted even more loudly, "Have mercy on us, Lord, Son of David!" Jesus stood still and called them, saying, "What do you want me to do for you?"

Pause for silent reflection. After this, allow time for participants to briefly mention their needs and those of others. Then let someone read aloud the conclusion of the Gospel episode (20:33–34):

They said to him, "Lord, let our eyes be opened." Moved with compassion, Jesus touched their eyes. Immediately they regained their sight and followed him.

End by praying an Our Father together.

A Living Tradition

The Picture on the Coin

This section is a supplement for individual reading.

In his fourth-century commentary on Matthew's Gospel, St. Jerome included two views on the parable of the vineyard workers that were circulating among Christians in his day. They have remained popular ever since.

It seems to me the workers of the first hour are Samuel and Jeremiah and John the Baptist, who can say with the psalmist, "From my mother's womb you are my God" (see Psalm 22:9–10). But the workers of the third hour are those who began to serve God from their youth; of the sixth hour, those who in mature age undertook the yoke of Christ; of the ninth, those already declining into old age; of the eleventh, those at the end of old age.

There are some who argue for a different interpretation of this parable. The workers of the first hour they prefer to interpret as Adam and the other patriarchs up to Noah; the third hour, Noah himself up to Abraham and the circumcision given to him; the sixth, from Abraham up to Moses, when the law was given; the ninth, Moses himself and the prophets; the eleventh, the apostles and the peoples of the gentiles, of whom all are envious.

Jerome proposed an original interpretation of the payment that the owner gives to the workers. As another episode in Matthew's Gospel makes clear (22:19–21), the coin in the parable—the denarius—bore the image of Caesar, the king of Rome. Jerome takes this as a clue that the workers' reward symbolizes the image of the king of all, God. Thus their reward reflects the restoration in human beings of the likeness to God, which was marred by human sin. "The denarius bears the image of the king. 'Therefore,' the owner says to the complaining laborers, 'you have received the reward which I had promised you, that is, my image and likeness.'"

The complaining workers, Jerome explains, mistakenly think that they should have received more coins for their labor than the later workers received. But the gift of being transformed into God's image is obviously neither increased nor decreased by others receiving the same transformation.

Suggestions for Bible Discussion Groups

Like a camping trip, a Bible discussion group works best if you agree on where you're going and how you intend to get there. Many groups use their first meeting to talk over such questions and reach a consensus. Here is a checklist of issues, with bits of advice from people who have experience in Bible discussions. (A planning discussion will go more smoothly if the leaders have thought through the following issues beforehand.)

Agree on your purpose. Are you getting together to gain wisdom and direction for your lives? to finally get acquainted with the Bible? to support one another in following Christ? to encourage those who are exploring—or reexploring—the Church? for other reasons?

Agree on attitudes. For example: "We're all beginners here." "We're here to help one another understand and respond to God's word." "We're not here to offer counseling or direction to one another." "We want to read Scripture prayerfully." What do *you* wish to emphasize? Make it explicit!

Agree on ground rules. Barbara J. Fleischer, in her useful book *Facilitating for Growth,* recommends that a group clearly state its approach to the following:

- *Preparation.* Do we agree to read the material and prepare answers to the questions before each meeting?
- *Attendance.* What kind of priority will we give to our meetings?
- *Self-revelation.* Are we willing to help the others in the group gradually get to know us—our weaknesses as well as our strengths, our needs as well as our gifts?
- *Listening.* Will we commit ourselves to listening to one another?
- *Confidentiality.* Will we keep everything that is shared *with* the group *in* the group?
- *Discretion.* Will we refrain from sharing about the faults and sins of people who are not in the group?
- *Encouragement and support.* Will we give as well as receive?
- *Participation.* Will we give each person the time and opportunity to make a contribution?

You could probably take a pen and draw a circle around *listening* and *confidentiality.* Those two points are especially important.

The following items could be added to Fleischer's list:

◆ *Relationship with parish.* Is our group part of the adult faith-formation program? independent but operating with the express approval of the pastor? not a parish-based group?

◆ *New members.* Will we let new members join us once we have begun the six weeks of discussions?

Agree on housekeeping.

◆ *When will we meet?*

◆ *How often will we meet?* Meeting weekly or every other week is best if you can manage it. William Riley remarks, "Meetings once a month are too distant from each other for the threads of the last session not to be lost" *(The Bible Study Group: An Owner's Manual).*

◆ *How long will meetings run?*

◆ *Where will we meet?*

◆ *Is any setup needed?* Christine Dodd writes that "the problem with meeting in a place like a church hall is that it can be very soul-destroying," given the cold, impersonal feel of many church facilities. If you have to meet in a church facility, Dodd recommends doing something to make the area homey *(Making Scripture Work).*

◆ *Who will host the meetings?* Leaders and hosts are not necessarily the same people.

◆ *Will we have refreshments?* Who will provide them?

◆ *What about child care?* Most experienced leaders of Bible discussion groups discourage bringing infants or other children to adult Bible discussions.

Agree on leadership. You need someone to facilitate—to keep the discussion on track, to see that everyone has a chance to speak, to help the group stay on schedule. Rena Duff, editor of the newsletter *Sharing God's Word Today,* recommends having two or three people take turns leading the discussions.

It's okay if the leader is not an expert on the Bible. You have this booklet, and if questions come up that no one can answer, you can delegate a participant to do a little research between meetings. It's important for the leader to set an example of listening, to draw out the quieter members (and occasionally restrain the more vocal ones), to move the group on when it gets stuck, to remind the members of their agreements, and to summarize what the group is accomplishing.

Bible discussion is an opportunity to experience the fulfillment of Jesus' promise "Where two or three are gathered in my name, I am there among them" (Matthew 18:20). Put your discussion group in Jesus' hands. Pray for the guidance of the Spirit. And have a great time exploring God's word together!

Suggestions for Individuals

Y ou can use this booklet just as well for individual study as for group discussion. While discussing the Bible with other people can be a rich experience, there are advantages to reading on your own. For example:

◆ You can focus on the points that interest you most.

◆ You can go at your own pace.

◆ You can be completely relaxed and unashamedly honest in your answers to all the questions, since you don't have to share them with anyone!

My suggestions for using this booklet on your own are these:

◆ Don't skip the Questions to Begin. The questions can help you as an individual reader warm up to the topic of the reading.

◆ Take your time on the Questions for Careful Reading and Questions for Application. While a group will probably not have enough time to work on all the questions, you can allow yourself the time to consider all of them if you are using the booklet by yourself.

◆ After reading the Guide to the Reading, go back and reread the Scripture text before answering the Questions for Application.

◆ Take the time to look up all the parenthetical Scripture references in the introduction, the Guides to the Readings, and the other material.

◆ Read the sections of Matthew's Gospel, chapters 10 through 20, that are omitted in this guide.

◆ Since you control the pace, give yourself plenty of opportunities to reflect on the meaning of Matthew's Gospel for you. Let your reading be an opportunity for these words to become God's words to you.

Bibles

The following editions of the Bible contain the full set of biblical books recognized by the Catholic Church, along with a great deal of useful explanatory material:

◆ The Catholic Study Bible (Oxford University Press), which uses the text of the New American Bible
◆ The Catholic Bible: Personal Study Edition (Oxford University Press), which also uses the text of the New American Bible
◆ The New Jerusalem Bible, the regular (not the reader's) edition (Doubleday)

Books

◆ George T. Montague, S.M., *Companion God: A Cross-Cultural Commentary on the Gospel of Matthew* (New York: Paulist Press, 1989).
◆ John P. Meier, *Matthew,* New Testament Message, vol. 3 (Collegeville, Minn.: Liturgical Press, 1990; originally published in 1980 by M. Glazier).

How has Scripture had an impact on your life? Was this booklet helpful to you in your study of the Bible? Please send comments, suggestions, and personal experiences to Kevin Perrotta, General Editor, Trade Editorial Department, Loyola Press, 3441 N. Ashland Ave., Chicago, IL 60657.